CONTENTS

EQUIPMENT

The examples in this book were made using Avenue Mandarine paper.

BASIC FOLDS

double triangle

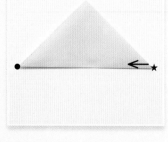

1 Position your paper like this. Fold the ★ onto the ● to make a triangle.

2 Fold the ★ onto the ● to make a smaller triangle.

3 And there you have your basic fold! You'll find that many creations begin with this fold.

4

squared rectangle

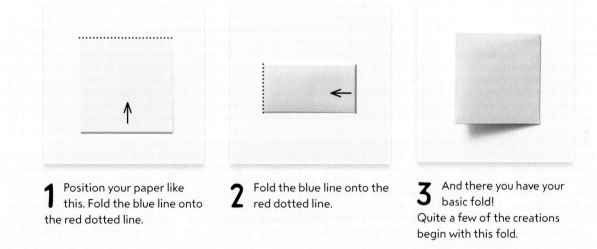

1 Position your paper like this. Fold the blue line onto the red dotted line.

2 Fold the blue line onto the red dotted line.

3 And there you have your basic fold!
Quite a few of the creations begin with this fold.

ice cream cone

1 Position your paper like this. Fold the ★ onto the ● to make a triangle.

2 Unfold this step.

3 Rotate your paper as shown in the picture. Fold the blue lines on each side onto the red dotted line in the middle.

4 And there you have your basic fold! You'll find that many creations begin with this fold.

BASIC FOLDS

pyramid

1 Position your paper like this. Fold the ★ onto the ● to make a triangle.

2 Fold the ★ onto the ● to make a smaller triangle.

3 Unfold the last step and fold the blue line onto the red dotted line in the middle.

4 Turn over your origami, as shown in the picture. Fold the blue line onto the red dotted line.

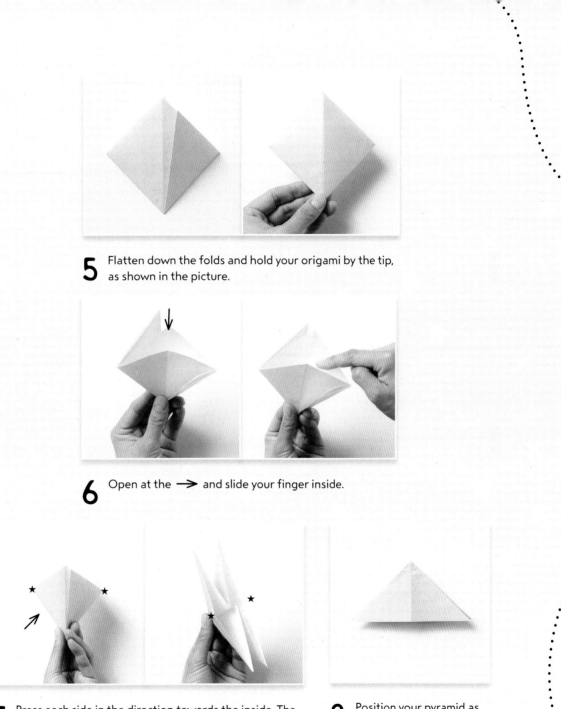

5 Flatten down the folds and hold your origami by the tip, as shown in the picture.

6 Open at the ➔ and slide your finger inside.

7 Press each side in the direction towards the inside. The two ★ should meet.

8 Position your pyramid as show in the picture. Make sure your fold is symmetrical.

BASIC FOLDS

diamond

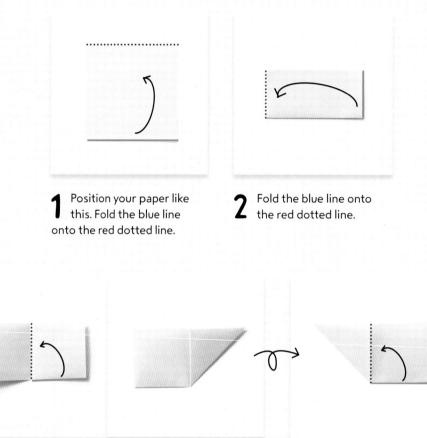

1 Position your paper like this. Fold the blue line onto the red dotted line.

2 Fold the blue line onto the red dotted line.

3 Unfold the last step and then fold the blue line onto the red dotted line.

4 Turn over your origami, as shown in the picture, and fold the blue line onto the red dotted line.

5 Smooth out the folds and hold it by the tip, as shown in the picture.

6 Open at the → and slide your finger inside.

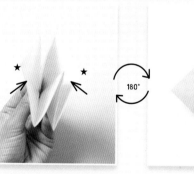

7 Fold at the → towards the inside—the 2 points marked ★ should meet.

8 Rotate your diamond as shown in the picture. Make sure your fold is symmetrical.

key to SYMBOLS

Folds

mountain fold

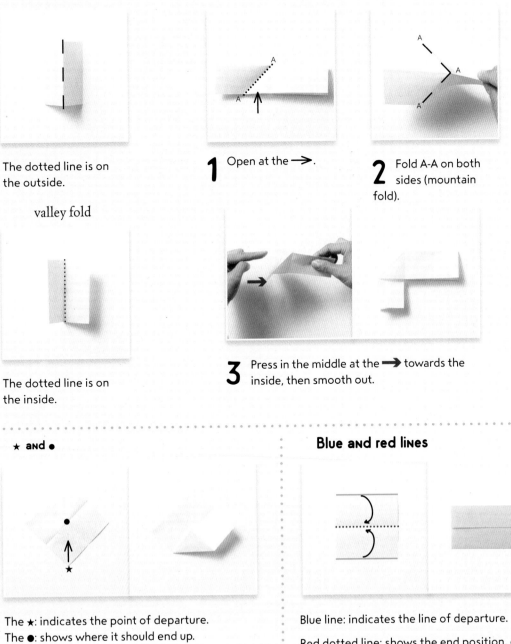

The dotted line is on the outside.

valley fold

The dotted line is on the inside.

inverted inside fold

1 Open at the ➡.

2 Fold A-A on both sides (mountain fold).

3 Press in the middle at the ➡ towards the inside, then smooth out.

★ and ●

The ★: indicates the point of departure.
The ●: shows where it should end up.

Blue and red lines

Blue line: indicates the line of departure.

Red dotted line: shows the end position, often the middle of the paper.

Rotate

Rotate.

Rotate 180°.

Cut

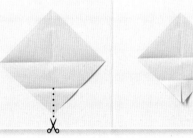

Cut.

Turn the paper over

Turn your origami over.

Open

Slide your finger inside to fully open.

Press

Press as shown in the picture.

ANIMAL HEADS

DOG head

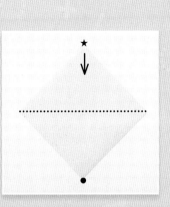

1 Fold your paper along the dotted center line, placing the ★ corner onto the ●: making a triangle.

2 Fold each side along the dotted line to create the dog's ears.

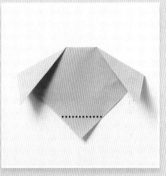

3 Fold upwards along the dotted line (only one layer).

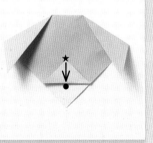

4 Fold the ★ onto the ● for the muzzle.

5 Fold back along the dotted line.

6 Now draw on your dog's eyes!

13

CAT head

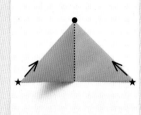

1 Start with the "double triangle" basic fold shown on page 4.

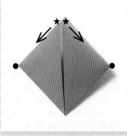

2 Unfold the last step and position your origami with the point at the top. Fold each ★ onto the ●.

3 Fold the two ★ onto their corresponding ●.

 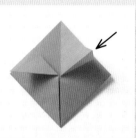 

4 Lift up the point marked with ●, open up at the → sliding your finger inside the pocket, and press underneath to create your cat's ears.

5 Do the same on the other side to form the second ear.

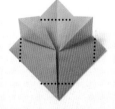  

6 Fold each side inwards along the dotted lines.

7 Turn your origami over. Now, draw on your cat's eyes!

14

RABBIT head

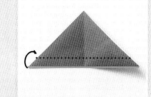

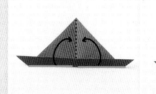

1 Start with the "double triangle" basic fold shown on page 4.

2 Unfold the last step of this fold and position your origami with the point at the top. Fold the blue line onto the red dotted line—you'll then have a boat shape.

3 Fold the blue lines on each side onto the red dotted line in the center. This will form your rabbit's ears.

4 Fold each side inwards along the dotted lines.

5 Turn your origami over. Fold down along the dotted line to round out the rabbit's head.

6 Draw on your rabbit's eyes!

FOX head

1 Start with the "double triangle" basic fold shown on page 4.

2 Unfold the last step and position the triangle in front of you, pointing upwards.
Fold the ★ onto the ●.

 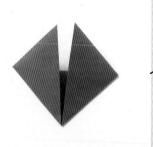 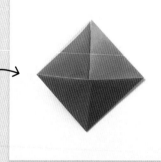

3 Fold the blue lines on each side onto the red dotted line in the middle

4 Turn your origami over. Now, draw on your fox's eyes!

DEER head

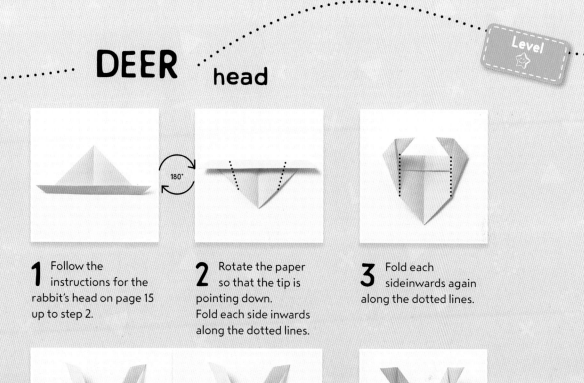

1 Follow the instructions for the rabbit's head on page 15 up to step 2.

2 Rotate the paper so that the tip is pointing down. Fold each side inwards along the dotted lines.

3 Fold each side inwards again along the dotted lines.

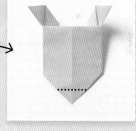

4 Fold upwards along the dotted line (only one layer).

5 Turn your origami over, then fold upwards along the dotted line.

6 Fold the ★ onto the ● to form the muzzle.

7 Now, draw on your deer's eyes!

rabbit

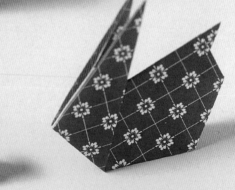

tree

RABBIT

1 Start with the "ice cream cone" basic fold shown on page 5. Fold the ★ onto the ● in the center.

2 Fold upwards along the dotted line.

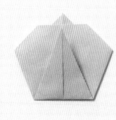

3 Turn your origami over. Fold the ★ onto the ●. You have a cupcake!

4 Turn your origami over. Fold from the middle towards you along the dotted line (valley fold).

5 Rotate your origami and position it as shown in the picture. Hold firmly at the ★, then pull the ears upwards. (Be careful not to bend them too much!)

6 Press firmly on the blue line.

7 Cut along the dotted line with some scissors to separate your rabbit's ears.

8 Open the ears fully— you have your rabbit!

TREE

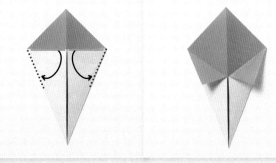

1 Position your paper pattern-side up and make the "ice cream cone" basic fold shown on page 5.

2 Fold the blue lines on each side onto the corresponding red dotted lines.

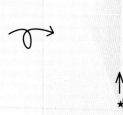

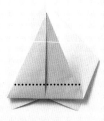

3 Turn your origami over. Fold the ★ onto the ●.

4 Fold towards you along the dotted line.

5 Fold the ★ onto the central ●.

6 Fold towards you along the dotted line.

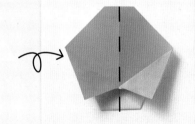

7 Turn your origami over—and there's your tree!
If you fold back along the dotted line (mountain fold), it will stand up by itself!

duck

DUCK

1 Start with the "ice cream cone" basic fold shown on page 5.

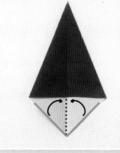

2 Rotate your origami 180°, as shown in the picture. Fold the blue lines on each side onto the red dotted line in the middle.

3 Fold along the dotted line towards the table (mountain fold).

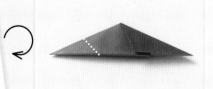

4 Rotate your origami 90°, as shown in the picture. Fold upwards along the dotted line, score the fold with your finger, then unfold it.

5 Open up at the →, then fold A-A on both sides (mountain fold).

DUCK continued

6 Press at ➡ the towards the inside, as shown in the picture (inverted inside fold, see page 10). Squeeze firmly on the bottom.

7 Fold downwards along the dotted line, score the fold, then unfold it.

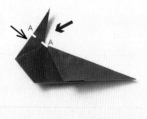

8 Open up at the ➡, then fold A-A on both sides (mountain fold). Press in the middle at the ➡ towards the inside, as shown in the picture (inverted inside fold, see page 10).

9 Fold upwards along the dotted line, score the fold, then unfold it.

10 Open at the ➜, then fold A-A on both sides (mountain fold). Press in the middle at the ➜ towards the inside, as shown in the picture (inverted inside fold, see page 10).

11 Fold downwards along the dotted line, score the fold, then unfold.

12 Open up at the ➜, then fold A-A on both sides (mountain fold). Press in the center at the ➜ (inverted inside fold, see page 10). Your duck is complete!

pig

dog

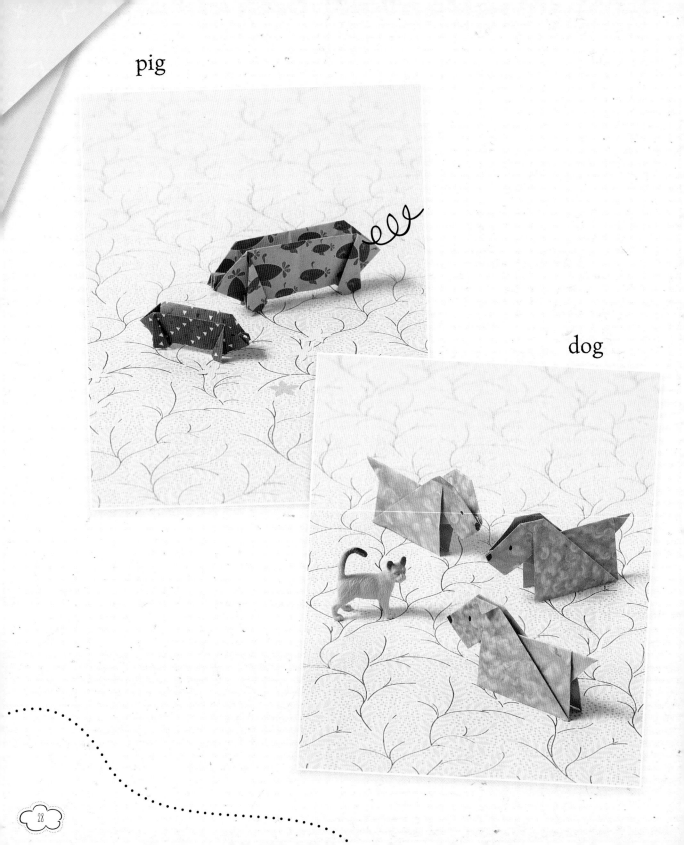

PIG

1 Start with the "double triangle" basic fold shown on page 4, then completely unfold.

2 Fold the paper in half to make a rectangle, then again to make a square.

3 Completely unfold. Fold the blue lines on each side onto the red dotted line in the middle.

4 Fold the blue lines on each side onto the red dotted line in the middle.
Score the folds.

PIG

continued

Level ★★★

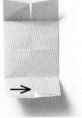 

5 Open at the →, put your finger inside, and fold the dotted lines in a mountain fold.

6 Do the same on all four sides, as shown in the picture.

7 Fold along the dotted line towards the table (mountain fold).

8 Rotate your origami as shown in the picture. Fold the blue lines on each side onto the corresponding central red dotted lines.

9 Fold upwards along the dotted line.

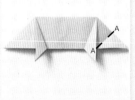

10 Unfold, then fold A-A along the dotted line on both sides (mountain fold).

11 Press at the ➡ towards the inside as shown in the picture (inverted inside fold, see page 10).

12 Fold upwards along the dotted line, and score the fold.

13 Unfold, then open at the ➡, and fold A-A on both sides (mountain fold).

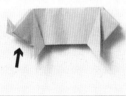

14 Press in the middle at the ➡ towards the inside as shown in the photo (inverted inside fold, see page 10), and finish the snout as shown in the following picture.

15 Fold inward along the dotted lines to form the 4 legs (mountain fold).
Your pig is finished!

DOG

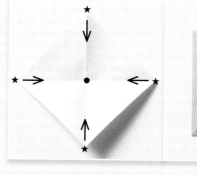

1 Start with the "double triangle" basic fold shown on page 4, then completely unfold.

2 Fold the 4 corners marked with ★ in to the center ●.

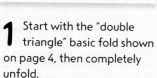

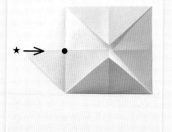

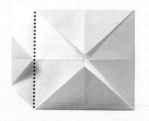

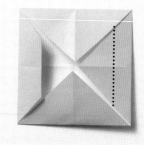

3 Unfold the section on the left, then fold the ★ onto the ●.

4 Fold to the right along the dotted line.

5 Fold to the right along the dotted line.

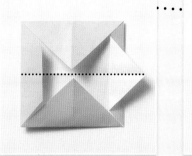

6 Fold downwards along the dotted line.

7 Fold upwards and diagonally along the dotted line.

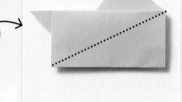

8 Turn over your origami, as shown in the picture. Fold upwards and diagonally along the dotted line.

9 Open up at the ➜ and pull out the folds hidden inside.

10 You've just made its paws!

11 Pull out the muzzle that is hidden inside.

12 Fold the ears on each side and draw your dog's eyes and nose!

MOUSE

Level
⭐⭐⭐

1 Start with the "double triangle" basic fold shown on page 4, then completely unfold.

2 Then do the "ice cream cone" basic fold shown on page 5.

180°

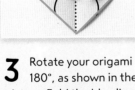

3 Rotate your origami 180°, as shown in the picture. Fold the blue lines on each side onto the red dotted line in the middle.

4 Carefully open up each side.

5 Fold the dotted lines into a mountain fold (see page 10), then pull them upwards.

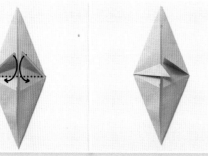

6 Fold the blue lines on each side onto the red dotted line in the middle.

  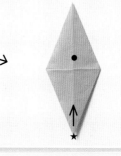

7 Fold the ★ onto the ●.

8 Turn your origami over, then fold the ★ onto the ●. (Be aware: this is not the center line!)

9 Fold the blue lines on each side onto the red dotted line in the middle.

10 Fold along the dotted line towards the inside (valley fold).

11 Rotate your origami as shown in the picture. Fold back along the dotted lines on each side to form the ears.

12 Fold downwards along the dotted line and score the fold.

13 Unfold this part and open up at the →, then press in the middle at the → towards the inside, as shown in the picture (inverted inside fold, see page 10).

14 Fold upwards along the dotted line, score the fold, then unfold it and open up at the →.

15 Press in the middle at the → towards the inside, as shown in the picture (inverted inside fold, see page 10). Finish off the tail and draw your mouse's eyes!

fish

penguin

honk, honk!

FISH

1 Start with the "double triangle" basic fold shown on page 4, then completely unfold.

2 Fold the ★ onto the ●.

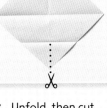

3 Unfold, then cut along the dotted line.

4 Rotate your origami as shown in the picture, then fold the blue line onto the red dotted line in the middle.

5 Fold towards you along the dotted line.

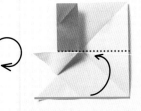

6 Rotate your origami as shown in the picture, then fold the blue line onto the red dotted line in the middle.

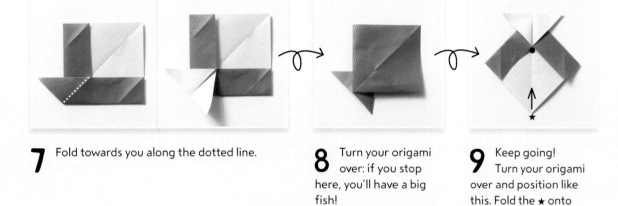

7 Fold towards you along the dotted line.

8 Turn your origami over: if you stop here, you'll have a big fish!

9 Keep going! Turn your origami over and position like this. Fold the ★ onto the ●.

10 Fold the blue lines on each side onto the red dotted line in the middle.

11 Turn your origami over and position like this. Now draw some patterns on your fish!

PENGUIN

1 Start with the "ice cream cone" basic fold shown on page 5. Fold the ★ onto the ●.

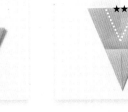

2 Unfold this step, then fold along the dotted line. The corners marked with ★ on each side must touch the outer edge as shown in the following picture.

3 Fold the ★ onto the ●.

4 Folding along the dotted line, bring the ★ to the bottom.

5 Then fold upwards along the dotted line.

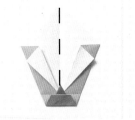

6 Fold back along the dotted line (mountain fold).

42

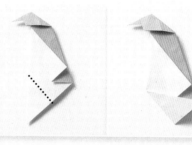

7 Rotate your origami 180° as shown in the picture. Hold firmly at the ★ then pull the head upwards (be careful not to fold too much!)

8 Fold upwards along the dotted line, score the fold, then unfold it.

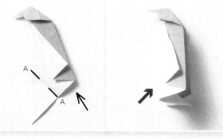

9 Open up at the ➔, then fold A-A on both sides (mountain fold). Press in the middle towards the inside, as shown in the picture (inverted inside fold, see page 10).

10 Fold upwards along the dotted line. Score the fold well.

11 Draw on your penguin's eyes!

crab

CRAB

1 Follow the instructions for the magic boat on page 68 up to step 7.

2 Fold the blue lines on each side onto the corresponding red dotted line.

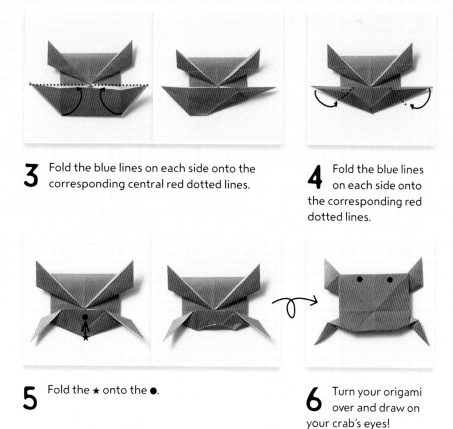

3 Fold the blue lines on each side onto the corresponding central red dotted lines.

4 Fold the blue lines on each side onto the corresponding red dotted lines.

5 Fold the ★ onto the ●.

6 Turn your origami over and draw on your crab's eyes!

45

whale

a boat and a skiff

WHALE

1 Start with the "double triangle" basic fold shown on page 4, then completely unfold.

2 Fold the blue line onto the central red dotted line.

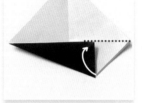

3 Fold the blue line onto the central red dotted line.

4 Slightly open up at the →.

5 Turn this dotted line into a mountain fold. Pull out towards the left.

6 Fold the ★ to the right.

7 Fold the blue line onto the red dotted line in the middle.

 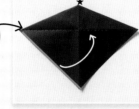 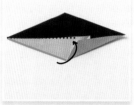

8 You've just made your whale's fin! Turn your origami over. (Note: the point marked with ★ is the same as the ★ in the following picture.)

9 Fold the blue line onto the central red dotted line.

10 Fold the blue line onto the central red dotted line.

11 Fold the blue line onto the central red dotted line.

12 Fold along the dotted lines towards the inside (valley fold).

13 Turn your origami over.
Now draw its eye!

BOAT

Level ⭐⭐

1 Start with the "diamond" basic fold shown on page 8. Fold the ★ (only one layer) onto the ●.

2 Fold both ★ onto the ●.

 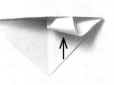

3 Slide the ends marked with ★ into the pocket, as show in the picture below.

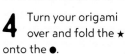

4 Turn your origami over and fold the ★ onto the ●.

5 Open up the triangle at the ➜, bring the two ends marked ★ to the other ★.

6 You have a square. Rotate your origami as shown in the picture.

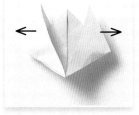

7 Pull each side out—don't be afraid to pull firmly.

8 Press firmly along the dotted line.

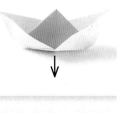

9 Open the boat at the ➜ so that it will stand up.

SKIFF

Level ☆☆

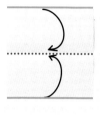

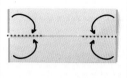

1 Fold in half along the dotted line, then unfold.

2 Fold the blue lines on each side onto the red dotted line in the middle.

3 Fold the blue lines on each side onto the corresponding red dotted lines.

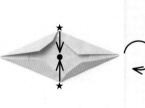

4 Fold the blue lines on each side onto the corresponding central red dotted lines.

5 Fold each ★ onto the ● in the center.

6 Rotate your origami as shown in the picture, and open up the middle dotted line at the towards the outside.

7 Open it up further.

8 Gently turn over the edges, until the boat is inverted.

9 Turn your origami over. You have made a skiff!

FUN OBJECTS

crane

spinning top

CRANE

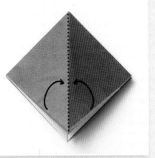

1 Start with the "diamond" basic fold shown on page 8. Fold the blue lines on either side onto the red dotted line to create a small ice cream cone.

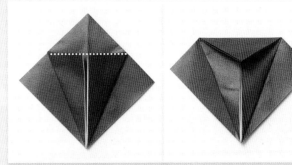

2 Fold downwards along the dotted line.

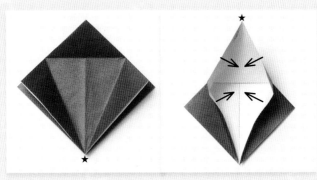

3 Unfold the previous 2 steps. Take hold of one layer at the tip marked ★ and pull upwards until it reaches the ★ at the top of the picture.

Level ☆☆☆

4 Clearly mark the blue line.

5 Turn your origami over and do steps 1 and 2 on this side. Then, unfold these 2 steps.

6 Next, redo steps 3 and 4.

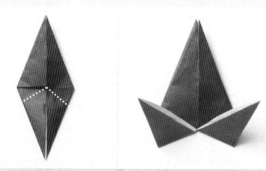

7 Fold upwards along the dotted line.

8 Unfold the last step, then open up at the →, and fold A-A on both sides (mountain fold).

9 Press in the middle at the → towards the inside (inverted inside fold, see page 10). Do the same on the right side.

10 Fold downwards along the dotted line.

11 Unfold this last step and do the inverted inside fold to form the beak.

12 Fold downwards along the dotted line. Turn your origami over and do the same thing on the other side.

How to PLAY with it!

Hold at the ● and pull outwards at the ★. Your crane will fly!

SPINNING TOP

1 Start by doing the "squared rectangle" basic fold shown on page 5 twice. Unfold one step.

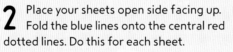

2 Place your sheets open side facing up. Fold the blue lines onto the central red dotted lines. Do this for each sheet.

3 Turn your origamis over, then rotate them and position them as shown in the picture.

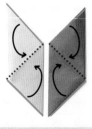 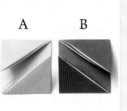

4 Fold the blue lines onto the red dotted lines. Do this for each sheet.

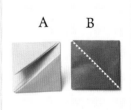

5 Turn over origami B, and position it as shown in the picture. Note: the dotted line should be diagonal.

6 Place origami B on top of A as shown in the picture.

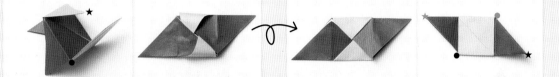

7 Slide the tip marked ★ into origami B until it reaches the ●. Do the same thing with the other tip and flatten down.

8 Turn your origami over, and slide the tip marked ★ into origami A until it reaches the ● (★ - ● / ★ - ●).

9 Flatten down well.

10 Using a toothpick and thumbtack, poke a hole in the middle of your spinning top using the thumbtack, then push the toothpick through it. If it isn't secure, use a little liquid glue.

How to PLAY with it!

Spin your spinner by rotating the wooden stick!

big mouth

BIG MOUTH

1 Fold in half along the central dotted line (valley fold).

2 Fold in half again along the central dotted line (valley fold).

3 Unfold completely, then fold the blue lines onto the red dotted lines on each side.

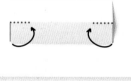

4 Fold along the dotted line (valley fold).

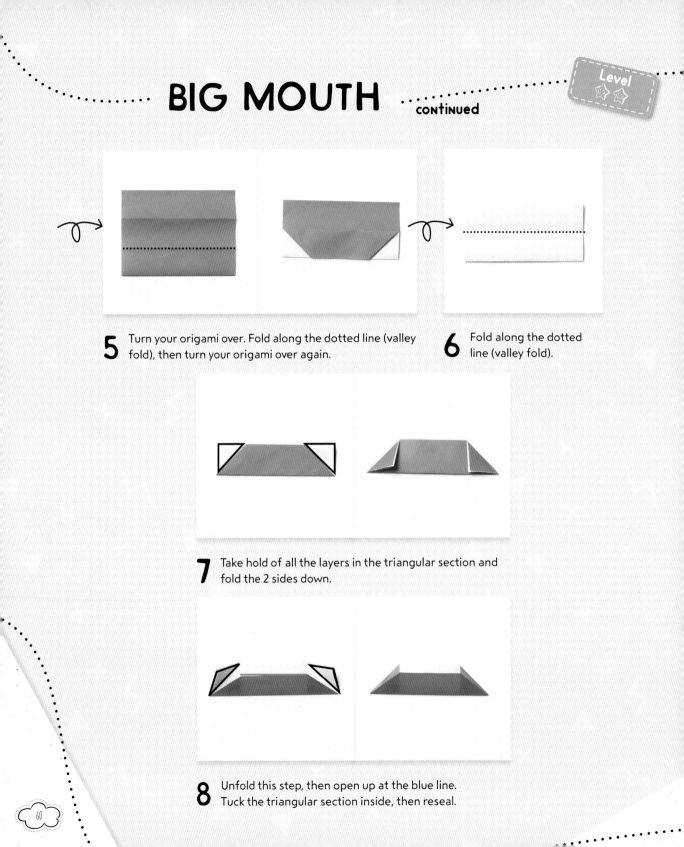

5 Turn your origami over. Fold along the dotted line (valley fold), then turn your origami over again.

6 Fold along the dotted line (valley fold).

7 Take hold of all the layers in the triangular section and fold the 2 sides down.

8 Unfold this step, then open up at the blue line. Tuck the triangular section inside, then reseal.

Slide your thumb and index finger into each side of the big mouth and have fun opening and closing it!

9 Position your origami so that it looks like a boat, as shown in the picture. Fold in half along the central dotted line (valley fold).

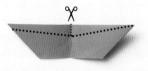 

10 Unfold this step, then cut along the center line (with scissors). Fold along the dotted line on both sides (valley fold).

11 Turn your origami over and do the same thing on the other side.

12 Open up at the →, and press in the middle at the → towards the inside. Draw eyes and teeth on your big mouth!

horse

neigh!

HORSE

1 Start with the "diamond" basic fold shown on page 8. Fold the blue lines on either side onto the red dotted line to create a small ice cream cone.

2 Fold downwards along the dotted line, then unfold the last 3 folds.

3 Cut along the line up to the ●.

4 Fold only the top layer along the dotted line, just like for the fox's head.

Level

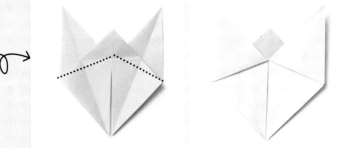

5 Turn your origami over and do steps 2–5 on this side. You'll have a fox's heads on both sides.

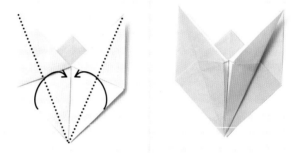

6 Fold towards the inside along the dotted line.

7 Turn your origami over and do the same thing on the other side.

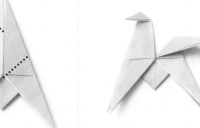

8 Rotate your origami 180°, as shown in the picture. Fold downwards along the dotted lines, then unfold both

9 Open up at the ➡, then fold A-A on both sides (mountain fold). Press in the middle at the ➡ towards the inside (inverted inside fold, see page 10) to form your horse's head.

10 Open up at the , then fold A-A on both sides (mountain fold). Press in the middle at the towards the inside (inverted inside fold, see page 10) to make the tail. Your horse is finished! Spread its legs out a little so that it will stand on its own.

How to PLAY with it!

To play with your horse, place your finger under its tail and flick it upwards. It will do a full somersault in the air!

magic boat

shuriken

MAGIC
BOAT

Level ☆☆ ☆☆

1 Start by doing the "double triangle" basic fold shown on page 4.

2 Completely unfold, then do the "diamond" basic fold shown on page 8.

3 Completely unfold. Fold the blue lines onto the central red dotted lines.

4 Fold the blue lines onto the central red dotted lines.

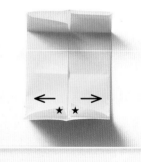

5 Unfold the last step. Pull the corners marked ★ towards the outside to make a boat. The tips marked ★ here are the same as those marked ★ on the next picture.

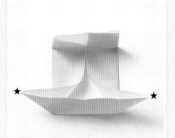

6 Do the same on both sides.

7 Fold the blue lines on each side onto the red dotted line in the middle.

8 Turn your origami over. Fold downwards along the dotted line.

9 You'll have a boat. Try folding the tip marked ★ on both sides.

10 It changes the orientation of the boat!

How to PLAY with it!

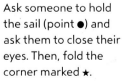

Ask someone to hold the sail (point ●) and ask them to close their eyes. Then, fold the corner marked ★.

This will change where the sail is. As them to open their eyes, then say: "I asked you to hold the sail!"

SHURIKEN

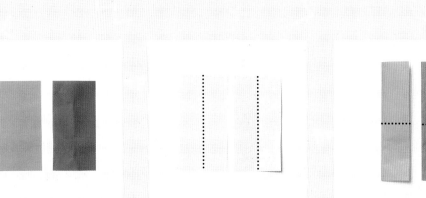

1 Prepare two half origami sheets and position them as shown in the photo. Turn them over.

2 Fold each sheet along the central dotted line.

3 Fold each sheet along the central dotted line.

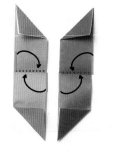

4 Unfold, then fold the blue lines onto the red dotted lines.

5 Fold the blue lines onto the red dotted lines.

6 You'll have four triangles.

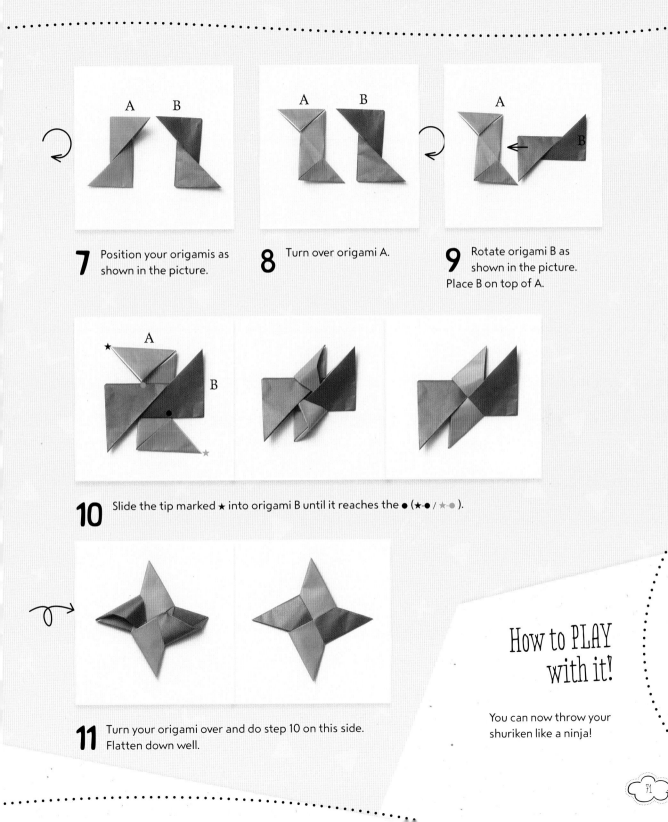

7 Position your origamis as shown in the picture.

8 Turn over origami A.

9 Rotate origami B as shown in the picture. Place B on top of A.

10 Slide the tip marked ★ into origami B until it reaches the ● (★-● / ★-●).

11 Turn your origami over and do step 10 on this side. Flatten down well.

How to PLAY with it!

You can now throw your shuriken like a ninja!

frog

hop, hop!

rabbit balloon

FROG

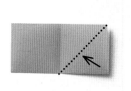

1 Start with the "diamond" basic fold shown on page 8. Unfold one step.

2 Fold upwards along the dotted line.

3 Unfold this step, then fold downwards along the dotted line.

4 Unfold this step, then turn your origami over.

5 Position it as shown in the picture, then press in the middle at the ➡ towards the inside.

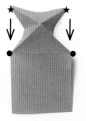

6 Fold the two ★ onto their corresponding ●.

7 Turn your origami over and you'll have a house! Fold the blue line onto the red dotted line.

8 Now you have a little house! Fold towards the inside along the dotted line.

9 Unfold this step, then fold the blue line onto the red dotted line.

10 Flatten down the center.

   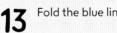 

11 Fold upwards along the dotted line.

12 Fold upwards along the dotted line.

13 Fold the blue line onto the red dotted line.

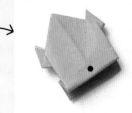

14 Turn your origami over and your frog is finished! With your index finger, pull the ● towards you.

How to PLAY with it!

To make your frog jump, press on its butt with your index finger and it will jump forward!

RABBIT
BALLOON

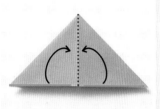

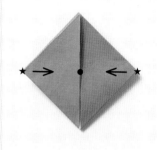

1 Start with the "pyramid" basic fold shown on page 6. Fold the blue lines on each side onto the red dotted line in the middle.

2 Score the folds well. Turn your origamiover and do the same thing on the other side.

3 Fold each ★ onto the central ●.

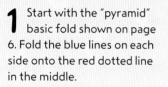

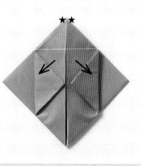

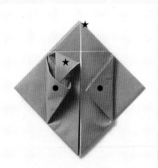

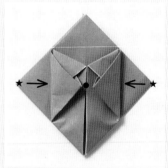

4 Open at the ➔ then put your finger inside the little pocket.

5 Slide the tips marked ★ into their corresponding pockets marked ●. Position them as shown in the next picture.

6 Fold each ★ onto the ● in the center.

This rabbit is a lot of fun: blow hard into the hole, and it will inflate like a balloon! Don't forget to draw its eyes!

7 Tuck the triangle you just made under the two layers on each side.

8 Turn your origami over. Fold towards the outside along the dotted lines.
You've made your rabbit's ears!

9 Blow inside at the ⟶ to inflate the balloon.

DECORATIONS

box

yum!

BOX

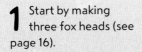

1 Start by making three fox heads (see page 16).

2 Unfold each origami and position them pointing downwards, as shown in the picture.

3 Slide the blue triangle on one origami into its neighbor's red triangle.

4 Start with two origamis, sliding the blue triangle into the red triangle, as shown in the picture.

5 Slide completely inside.

6 Do the same thing with the second and then the third.

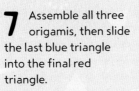

7 Assemble all three origamis, then slide the last blue triangle into the final red triangle.

8 Fit together carefully and glue the base. You have your box!

butterfly

flower

BUTTERFLY

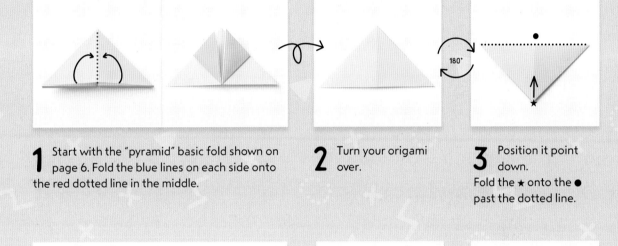

1 Start with the "pyramid" basic fold shown on page 6. Fold the blue lines on each side onto the red dotted line in the middle.

2 Turn your origami over.

3 Position it point down. Fold the ★ onto the ● past the dotted line.

4 Fold the overlapping part backwards (the blue triangle).

5 Turn your origami over. Fold along the dotted line in a valley fold (see page 10) and press firmly.

6 Now your butterfly can fly away!

FLOWER

1 Prepare five origami sheets measuring 3x3 inches.

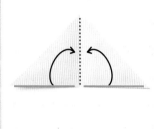

2 Start with the "triangle" basic fold shown on page 4, then completely unfold.

3 Fold the blue lines onto the central red dotted line.

4 Slightly lift the blue lines on each side towards you.

5 Open up at the → on both sides and put your finger inside the little pocket.

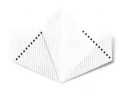

6 Press down firmly on the folds on both sides, as shown in the picture. Fold downwards along the dotted lines.

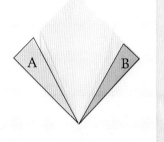

7 Fold the blue lines on each side onto the corresponding red dotted lines.

8 Stick the parts marked A and B together.

9 You've made a petal.

10 Make five petals in the same way and leave them to dry.

11 Stick the five petals together facing the same direction.

12 Use a paper clip to help them stick. Wait a few moments before removing it.

13 Carefully open up the petals and glue the last piece. Hold this last piece together with the paper clip and wait a few minutes until it holds in a circular flower shape. Your flower is finished!

garland

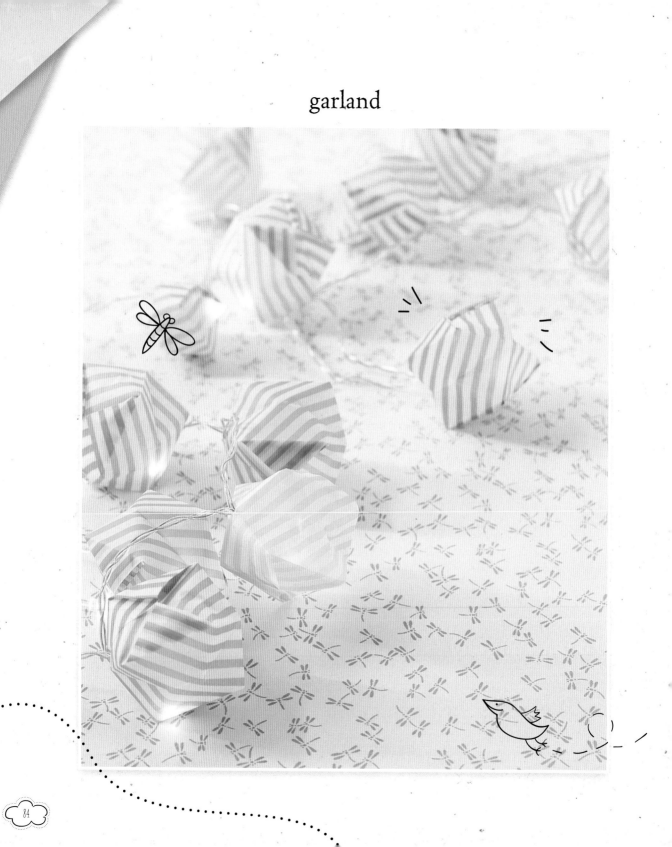

GARLAND

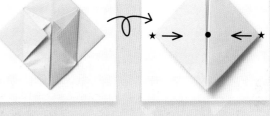

1 Start with the "pyramid" basic fold shown on page 6.

2 Follow the instructions for the rabbit balloon (see page 76) up to step 6.

3 Turn your origami over. Fold the two ★ onto the center ●.

4 On each side, slide the tips marked ★ into the pockets marked ●. Position them as shown in the next picture.

5 Separate the four layers.

6 Blow inside at the → (there's a small hole) to inflate the origami.

7 Make several of these balls and slip a thread through the holes to form a garland.

HEARTS

simple heart

bookmark

SIMPLE
HEART

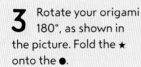

1 Start with the "pyramid" basic fold shown on page 16, then unfold.

2 Fold the corner marked ★ onto the ●.

3 Rotate your origami 180°, as shown in the picture. Fold the ★ onto the ●.

4 Fold the blue lines on each side onto the red dotted line in the middle. Fold the ends to the inside in a triangle (mountain fold).

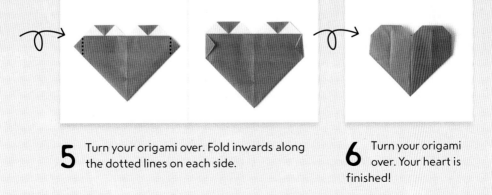

5 Turn your origami over. Fold inwards along the dotted lines on each side.

6 Turn your origami over. Your heart is finished!

BOOKMARK

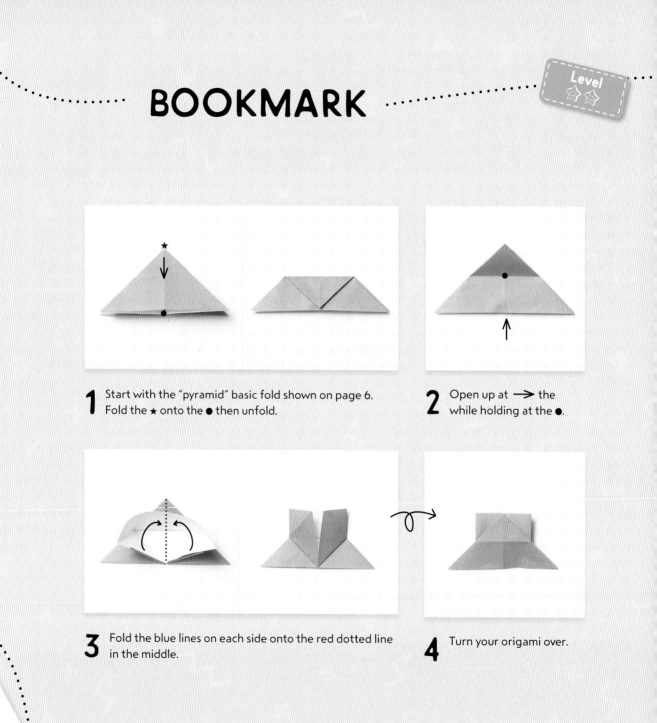

1 Start with the "pyramid" basic fold shown on page 6. Fold the ★ onto the ● then unfold.

2 Open up at → the while holding at the ●.

3 Fold the blue lines on each side onto the red dotted line in the middle.

4 Turn your origami over.

88

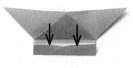

5 Rotate it 180°, as shown in the picture.
Fold the ★ onto the ●.

6 Fold the blue line onto the red dotted line in the middle.

7 Open up at the →.

8 Flatten down each side to make triangles, as shown in the next picture.

9 Fold the blue lines on each side onto the corresponding red dotted lines.

10 Fold upwards along the dotted line.

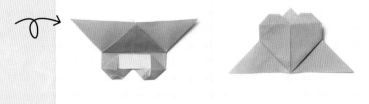

11 Turn your origami over, and position it as shown in the picture. You've finished your bookmark!

bracelet

winged heart

BRACELET

1 Start with the "squared rectangle" basic fold shown on page 5, using an 8x8 inch sheet of origami paper, then completely unfold.

2 Fold the blue line onto the red dotted line in the middle.

3 Unfold, then fold the blue line onto the red dotted line.

4 Fold upwards along the dotted line.

5 Turn your origami over. Fold the blue lines on each side onto the red dotted line in the middle.

6 Turn your origami over. Fold upwards along the dotted line.

7 Turn your origami over. Open up at the →.

8 Fold the blue lines onto the red dotted lines.

9 Fold the blue lines onto the central red dotted lines.

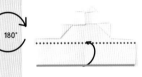

10 Rotate your origami 180°, as shown in the picture. Fold the blue line onto the red dotted line.

11 Fold the blue line onto the red dotted line in the middle.

12 Fold the blue line onto the red dotted line.

13 Turn your origami over. Now, shape into a circle to make your bracelet!

WINGED HEART

1
Start with the "squared rectangle" basic fold shown on page 5, then completely unfold.

2
Fold the blue line onto the red dotted line in the middle.

3
Turn your origami over. Fold the blue lines on each side onto the red dotted line in the middle.

4
Turn your origami over.

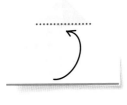

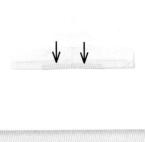

5 Rotate it 180°, as shown in the picture.
Fold the blue line onto the red dotted line in the middle.

6 Fold upwards along the dotted line.

7 Open up at the →.

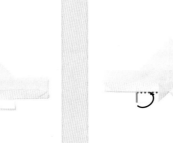

8 Flatten down each side to make triangles as shown in the next picture.

9 Fold the blue lines on each side onto the corresponding red dotted lines.

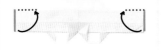 

10 Fold the blue lines on each side onto the corresponding red dotted lines.

11 Turn your origami over and position it as shown in the picture: your heart is finished!

Acknowledgments

Since I launched StudiOrigami, over 100 children have been making origami with me every week, in their schools, or other cultural establishments. I've improved greatly over the years in the way I explain the techniques, the way I fold the sheets, and in my choice of designs that are suited to their level and age. Their unfettered imaginations and the questions they ask me at each step have helped me develop my methodology and improve my workshops.

So, I would like to thank all the kids who have folded origami and had fun with me, for giving me all these ideas. It is thanks to them that I have been able to write this book, using explanations that are accessible to them.

Many thanks also to the photographer, Richard Boutin, and to my editor, Flore Beaugendre, as well as to all the people who have contributed to bringing this book to life.

Sayaka Hodoshima

Having relocated to France in 2001, Sayaka Hodoshima is still fascinated by the cultural diversity in this beautiful country, which reminds her of her native Japan.

After working as an interior designer in Bordeaux for eight years, she created her workshop, StudiOrigami, and now teaches origami in elementary schools, colleges, and libraries. She works in conjunction with architects and cultural mediators during educational and cultural workshops.

She is keen to share this activity with as many people as possible because she wants to contribute to the development of origami culture throughout France.

Her most cherished dream would be for you to join her in the playful and poetic world of origami!